What's for lunch?

Milk

This edition 2003

Franklin Watts
96 Leonard Street
London
EC2A 4XD

Franklin Watts Australia
45-51 Huntley Street
Alexandria
NSW 2015

Copyright © 1998 Franklin Watts

Editor: Samantha Armstrong
Series Designer: Kirstie Billingham
Consultant: National Dairy Council
Reading Consultant: Prue Goodwin, Reading and Language
Information Centre, Reading

A CIP catalogue record for this book is available from the British Library
Dewey Decimal Classification Number 637

ISBN: 0 7496 4936 4

Printed in Hong Kong, China

What's for lunch?

Milk

Claire Llewellyn

W

FRANKLIN WATTS

LONDON•SYDNEY

Today we are drinking milk with our lunch.
Milk is full of goodness.
It contains **proteins**, **vitamins** and **minerals**.
Milk gives us **energy** and helps us to grow
and stay healthy.

Most of the milk we drink
comes from cows on **dairy farms**.
Cows feed on grass, so dairy farms
are found in places where the grass grows
juicy and thick.

Cows are **mammals**.
Like all mammals,
they feed their young
on milk.
After giving birth to a calf,
a cow produces milk
in her **udder**.
She makes much more
than her calf needs.
We take some of the milk
and use it for ourselves.

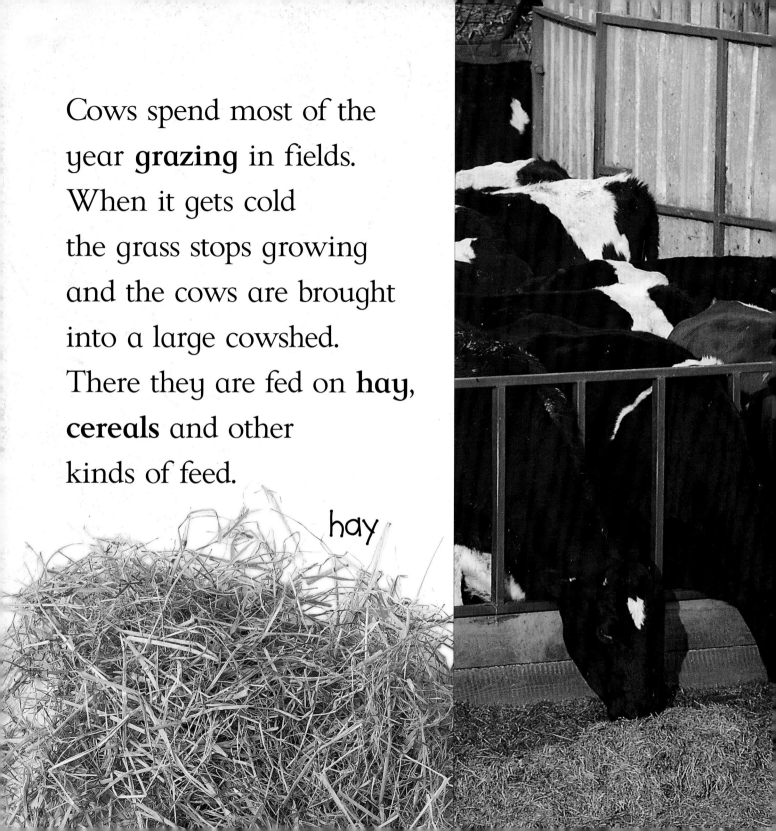

Cows spend most of the
year **grazing** in fields.
When it gets cold
the grass stops growing
and the cows are brought
into a large cowshed.
There they are fed on **hay**,
cereals and other
kinds of feed.

hay

Cows are usually milked twice a day -
once in the early morning
and again in the afternoon.
They are milked in a **milking parlour**.
Their udders are washed and dried
and then covered by four **teat cups**.
These squeeze the cows' udders very gently
and draw the milk into a container.

The milk is piped into a large, clean
storage tank called a **farm vat**.
The vat is **refrigerated** to keep the milk cool.

After milking, the farmer hoses down the parlour with water and makes sure that everything is spotlessly clean.

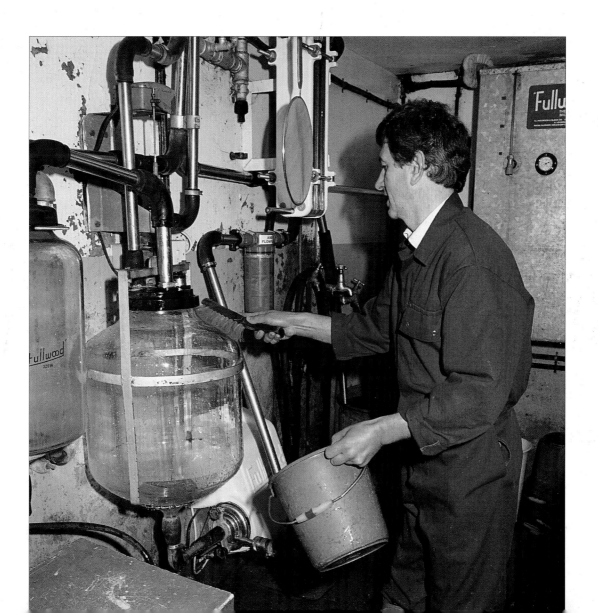

Every morning a tanker comes to collect the milk.
The driver connects a long hose to the vat, and
the milk is sucked up into the tanker.
The driver transports the milk to the **dairy**.

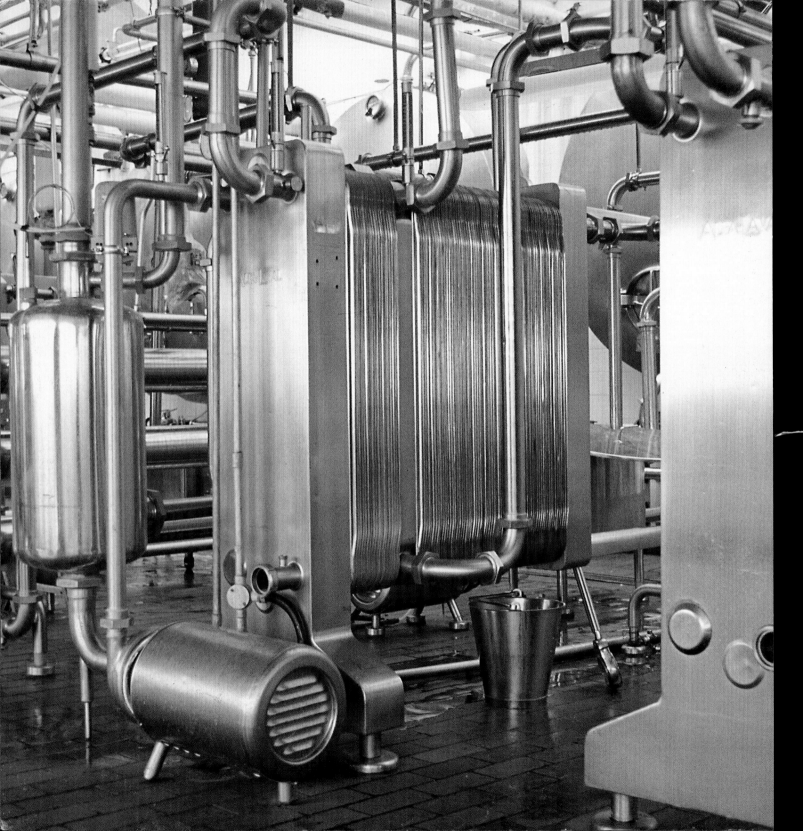

At the dairy, the milk is
specially treated to keep it fresh.
This treatment is called **pasteurization**.
Pasteurization is important
because it kills **bacteria**
that could harm us.

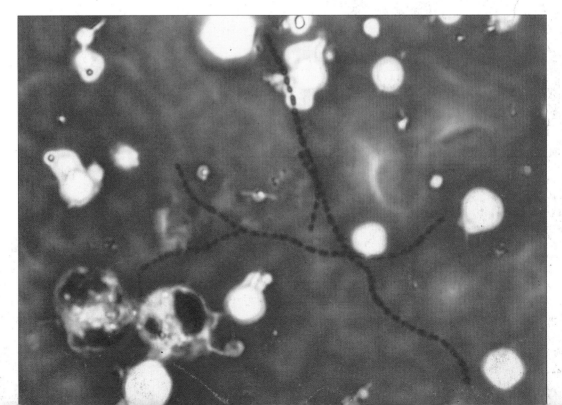

Cows' milk is very creamy.
Some people like all the cream
in their milk, some like just a little,
and others prefer none at all.
At the dairy the cream can be
skimmed off to make
semi-skimmed or skimmed milk.
The milk is put into bottles or
different coloured cartons.

The cartons are loaded onto lorries.
These are refrigerated to keep the milk fresh.
They deliver the milk to shops
for people to buy.

Not all milk ends up in cartons.
Some of it is delivered to factories,
called **creameries**, where butter
and different types of cheese are made.

Some milk is used to make yogurt.
Frozen cream is used
to make ice-cream.
Sometimes fruit and other flavours
are added to give yogurt and
ice-cream delicious tastes.

We use milk to cook sauces,
pancakes and puddings.
We also use it for milkshakes.
See how many ways you enjoy
milk every day!

Glossary

bacteria — tiny living things so small we can't see them that live all around us and can cause disease

creamery — a factory in which cheese and butter are made

cereal — a kind of plant, such as wheat, oats and barley, which is grown for its grains

dairy — a place where milk is processed

dairy farm — farms where cows are raised for their milk

energy — the strength to work and play

farm vat — a large container where milk is kept

graze — to feed on grass outside in fields

hay — dried grass

mammal — an animal, such as a cow, that gives birth to its young and feeds it on milk

milking parlour — the place where cows are taken to be milked

mineral	a material that is found in rocks and also in our food. Minerals are important for a healthy body
pasteurization	a way of heat treating milk that destroys harmful bacteria
protein	something found in foods, such as milk and meat, that helps to build our body and keep us healthy
refrigerate	make cool
skimmed	milk from which the cream has been removed
teat cups	suction cups that gently squeeze the milk from the cow's udder
udder	the part of the cow where milk is stored
vitamin	something found in milk, fruit and vegetables that keeps us healthy

Index

Picture credits: Bruce Coleman (Hans Reinhard) 8-9; Eye Ubiquitous (David Langfield) 21, 22; FLPA (Peter Dean) 6, 7, 10-11, 14, 15; Holt Studios International 13 (Nigel Cattlin), 24 (Inga Spence); Image Bank 16-17, 18 (Francesco Anggeri), 27 (Juan Silva); Oxford Scientific Films 19; Steve Shott cover; All other photographs Tim Ridley, Wells Street Studios, London. **With thanks to Roxanne Carney and Thomas Ong.**